I0412924

The Book of

Romantic Lines

Jessica Belle

For Eros

CONTENTS

"Romance is everything."

--Gertrude Stein

"Vulnerability is the essence of romance. It's the art of being uncalculated, the willingness to look foolish, the courage to say, 'This is me, and I'm interested in you enough to show you my flaws with the hope that you may embrace me for all that I am but, more important, all that I am not."

--Ashton Kutcher

Welcome to the Book of Romantic Lines. Here you will find the most romantic lines that will surely melt your hearts. Be it from the famous movies, from the timeless books, or from a person's heart.

MOVIES ROMANTIC LINES

Join me in this journey of nostalgia and let's reminisce to our beloved romantic movies that changed our lives from childhood until today.

"I could die right now, Clem. I'm just... happy. I've never felt that before. I'm just exactly where I want to be."

Joel, *Eternal Sunshine of the Spotless Mind* (2004)

"I would rather have had one breath of her hair, one kiss of her mouth, one touch of her hand than eternity without it. One."

-Seth, *City of Angels* (1998)

Donna: Will you still love me in the morning?

Michael: Forever and ever, babe.

Click (2006)

"I love you. You... you complete me."

Jerry Maguire, *Jerry Maguire* (1996)

"I don't think you're an idiot at all. I mean, there are elements of the ridiculous about you... you tend to let whatever's in your head come out of your mouth without much consideration of the consequences... But the thing is, um, what I'm trying to say, very inarticulately, is that, um, in fact, perhaps despite appearances, I like you, very much. Just as you are."

Mark Darcy, *Bridget Jones' Diary* (2001)

"Well, it was a million tiny little things that, when you added them all up, they meant we were supposed to be together. I knew it the very first time I touched her. I was just taking her hand to help her out of a car and I knew. It was like… magic."

Sam Baldwin, *Sleepless In Seattle* (1993)

"I came here tonight because when you realize you want to spend the rest of your life with somebody, you want the rest of your life to start as soon as possible."

Harry Burns, *When Harry Met Sally* (1989)

"Love is too weak a word for what I feel – I luuurve you, you know, I loave you, I luff you, two F's, yes I have to invent, of course I – I do, don't you think I do?"

Alvy Singer, *Annie Hall* (1977)

"I think technically 'The Girl Of My Dreams' would probably have like a really bodacious rack, you know, maybe different hair, she'd probably be a little more into sports. But truthfully, Robyn is better than the girl of my dreams. She's real."

Paul, *(500)Days Of Summer* (2009)

"I might be the only person on the face of the earth that knows you're the greatest woman on earth. I might be the only one who appreciates how amazing you are in every single thing that you do, and how you say what you mean, and how you almost always mean something that's all about being straight and good. I think most people miss that about you, and I watch them, wondering how they can watch you bring their food, and clear their tables and never get that they just met the greatest woman alive."

Melvin Udall, *As Good As It Gets* (1997)

"Our love is like the wind... I can't see it, but I sure can feel it."

Landon Carter, *A Walk to Remember* (2002)

"The only way you can beat my crazy was by doing something crazy yourself. Thank you. I love you. I knew it the minute I met you. I'm sorry it took so long for me to catch up. I just got stuck."

Pat, *Silver Linings Playbook* (2012)

"I'm scared of walking out of this room and never feeling the rest of my whole life the way I feel when I'm with you."

Baby, *Dirty Dancing* (1987)

"For now let me say, – without hope or agenda, – just because it's Christmas – and at Christmas you tell the truth – to me, you are perfect."

Mark, *Love Actually* (2003)

"Look, in my opinion, the best thing you can do is find a person who loves you for exactly what you are. Good mood, bad mood, ugly, pretty, handsome, what have you, the right person is still going to think the sun shines out your ass. That's the kind of person that's worth sticking with."

Mac Macguff, *Juno* (2007)

"My affections and wishes have not changed, but one word from you will silence me forever. If, however, your feelings have changed, I will have to tell you: you have bewitched me, body and soul, and I love, I love, I love you. I never wish to be parted from you from this day on."

Mr. Darcy, *Pride and Prejudice* (2005)

I am nothing special; just a common man with common thoughts, and I've led a common life. There are no monuments dedicated to me and my name will soon be forgotten. But in one respect I have succeeded as gloriously as anyone who's ever lived: I've loved another with all my heart and soul; and to me, this has always been enough.

Noah, *The Notebook* (2004)

"But for now, let me say — without hope or agenda, just because it's Christmas and at Christmas you tell the truth — to me, you are perfect. And my wasted heart will love you. Until you look like this [picture of a mummy]. Merry Christmas."

Mark, *Love Actually* (2003)

"You should be kissed and often, and by someone who knows how"

Rhett Butler, *Gone with the Wind* (1939)

"But you- You are what I never knew I always wanted."

Alex Whitman, Fools Rush In (1997)

"You make me want to be a better man."

Melvin Udall, *As Good as It Gets* (1997)

Princess Leia, "I love you."

Han Solo, "I know."

Star Wars: Episode V - The Empire Strikes Back (1980)

"It's a wonderful thing, as time goes by, to be with someone who looks into your face, when you've gotten old, and still sees what you think you look like."

Priest, *The Bachelor* (1999)

"I think I'd miss you even if we never met."

Nick Mercer, *The Wedding Date* (2005)

Jake, "Why do you want to marry me anyhow?" Melanie, "So I can kiss you anytime I want."

Sweet Home Alabama (2002)

"You had me at 'hello'."

Dorothy, *Jerry Maguire* (1996)

"I'd rather fight with you than make love with anyone else."

Nick Mercer, *The Wedding Date* (2005)

"I would rather spend one lifetime with you, than face all the ages of this world alone.

Arwen, *Lord of the Rings: The Fellowship of the Ring* (2001)

"Whatever you do in life will be insignificant, but it's very important that you do it. Because nobody else will. Like when someone comes into your life and half of you says you're nowhere near ready, but the other half says: make her yours forever."

Tyler, *Remember me* (2010)

"I know who you are, Sam. I know I'm quiet... and, and I know I should speak more. But if you knew the things that were in my head most of the time, you'd know what it really meant. How, how much we're alike, and how we've been through the same things... and you're not small. You're beautiful."

Charlie, *Perks of being a Wallflower* (2012)

"You died on a Saturday morning. And I had you placed here under our tree. And I had that house of your father's bulldozed to the ground. Momma always said dying' was a part of life. I sure wish it wasn't. Little Forrest, he's doing just fine. About to start school again soon. I make his breakfast, lunch, and dinner every day. I make sure he combs his hair and brushes his teeth every day. Teaching him how to play ping-pong. He's really good. We fish a lot. And every night, we read a book. He's so smart, Jenny. You'd be so proud of him. I am. He, uh, wrote a letter, and he says I can't read it. I'm not supposed to, so I'll just leave it here for you. Jenny, I don't know if Momma was right or if, if it's Lieutenant Dan. I don't know if we each have a destiny, or if we're all just floating around accidental-like on a breeze, but I, I think maybe it's both. Maybe both is happening at the same time. I miss you, Jenny. If there's anything you need, I won't be far away."

Forrest Gump, *Forrest Gump* (1994)

God: Grace. You want her back?

Bruce: No. I want her to be happy, no matter what that means. I want her to find someone who will treat her with all the love she deserved from me. I want her to meet someone who will see her always as I do now, through Your eyes.

God: Now THAT'S a prayer.

Bruce Almighty (2003)

Alexander Andrews: Do you love her?

Peter Warne: A normal human being couldn't live under the same roof with her without going nutty! She's my idea of nothing!

Alexander Andrews: I asked you a simple question! Do you love her?

Peter Warne: YES! But don't hold that against me, I'm a little screwy myself!

It Happened One Night (1934)

"I would rather have had one breath of her hair, one kiss of her mouth, one touch of her hand, than eternity without it. One."

Seth, *City of Angels* (1998)

"I have another scenario for you - I'm in love with you. I apologize for the blunt delivery, but as problematic as this fact may be, I'm in love... with YOU. I'm not feeling this because you're leaving, and not because it feels good to feel this way... which, by the way, it does, or did before you went off like that. I can't figure out the mathematics of this, I just know I love you. I can't believe how many times I'm saying it! And I never thought I'd feel this way again, so that's pretty phenomenal. And I realize that I come as a package deal: 3 for the price of 1. I know my package, perhaps in the light of day, isn't all that wonderful, but I finally know what I want and that, in itself, is a miracle. And what I want is YOU."

Graham, *The Holiday* (2006)

"I... am madly in love with you, Penny. You're my favorite, favorite thing."

Dodge Peterson, *Seeking a Friend for the End of the World* (2012)

"I wait all day, just hoping for one more minute with you, and I don't even know you."

Maggie Rice, *City of Angels* (1998)

George Malley: Hey, would you, uh, love me the rest of my life?

Lace Pennamin: No. I'm gonna love you for the rest of mine.

Phenomenon, 1996

Marian: You came for me... You're alive...

Robin Hood: I would die for you.

Robin Hood: Prince of Thieves (1991)

"I'm warning you, if you take one step closer, I'm never letting you go."

Adam, *No Strings Attached* (2011)

"Have I ever told you I love you?"

Diana, *Indecent Proposal* (1993)

"You are everything I never knew I always wanted."

Alex Whitman, *Fools Rush In* (1997)

"I-I've come here with no expectations, only to profess, now that I am at liberty to do so, that my heart is, and always will be, yours."

Edward Ferris, *Sense and Sensibility* (1995)

"After all... I'm just a girl, standing in front of a boy, asking him to love her."

Anna Scott, *Notting Hill* (1999)

"The greatest thing you'll ever learn is just to love and be loved in return."

Christian, *Moulin Rouge* (2001)

"I would have asked for your number, and I wouldn't have been able to wait twenty-four hours before calling you and saying, 'Hey, how about... oh, how about some coffee or, you know, drinks or dinner or a movie... for as long as we both shall live?'"

Joe Fox, *You've got mail* (1998)

"They say that when you meet the love of your life, time stops. And that's true."

Edward Bloom, *Big Fish* (2003)

"So it's not gonna be easy. It's going to be really hard; we're gonna have to work at this everyday, but I want to do that because I want you. I want all of you, forever, everyday. You and me... everyday."

Noah, *The Notebook* (2004)

"Come back with your shield, or on it."

Queen Gorgo, *300* (2006)

"I was unconditionally and irrevocably in love with him."

Isabella Swan, *Twilight* (2008)

"My heart will always belong to you."

Davy Jones, *Pirates of the Caribbean: Dead Man's Chest* (2006)

Luce: Don't forget me.

Rachel: I won't remember anything else.

Imagine Me & You (2005)

"Moral fiber. So, what is moral fiber? It's funny, I used to think it was always telling the truth, doing good deeds, basically [mumbling] being a fucking boy scout. But lately I've been seeing it differently. Now I think moral fiber's about finding that one thing you really care about. That one special thing that means more to you than anything else in the world. And when you find her, you fight for her. You risk it all, you put her in front of everything, your life, all of it. And maybe the stuff you do to help her isn't so clean. You know what? It doesn't matter. Because in your heart you know, that the juice is worth the squeeze. That's what moral fiber's all about."

Mathew Kidsman, *The Girl Next Door* (2004)

Jamal Malik: Come away with me.

Latika: Away? Where? And live on what?

Jamal: Love.

Slumdog Millionaire (2008)

"What I really want to do with my life - what I want to do for a living - is I want to be with your daughter. I'm good at it."

Lloyd Dobler, *Say Anything* (1989)

Samantha: Thanks for getting my undies back.

Jake: Thanks for coming over.

Samantha: Thanks for coming to get me.

Jake: Happy Birthday,

Samantha. Make a wish.

Samantha: It already came true.

Sixteen Candles (1984)

"All these years, all these memories, there was you. You pull me through time."

Tom Creo, *The Fountain* (2006)

"This kind of certainty comes but just once in a lifetime."

Robert Kincaid, *The Bridges of Madison County* (1995)

"My true disability is not having to be in a wheel chair. It's having to be without her."

Philippe, *Intouchables* (2011)

"We'll all become somebody's mom or dad. But right now these moments are not stories. This is happening. I am here and I am looking at her. And she is so beautiful. I can see it. This one moment when you know you're not a sad story. You are alive, and you stand up and see the lights on the buildings and everything that makes you wonder. And you're listening to that song and that drive with the people you love most in this world. And in this moment I swear, we are infinite."

Charlie, *Perks of Being a Wallflower* (2012)

"But, Gus, my love, I cannot tell you how thankful I am for our little infinity. I wouldn't trade it for the world. You gave me a forever within the numbered days, and I'm grateful."

Hazel Grace Lancaster, *The Fault in our Stars* (2014)

Landon: Do you love me?

[she nods]

Landon: Will you do something for me, then?

Jamie: [smiles] Anything.

Landon: Will you marry me?

A Walk to Remember (2002)

Paige: I vow to help you love life, to always hold you with tenderness and to have the patience that love demands, to speak when words are needed and to share the silence when they are not, to agree to disagree on red velvet cake, and to live within the warmth of your heart and always call it home.

Leo: I vow to fiercely love you in all your forms, now and forever. I promise to never forget that this is a once in a lifetime love. And to always know in the deepest part of my soul that no matter what challenges might carry us apart, we will always find our way back to each other.

The Vow (2012)

"My affections and wishes have not changed, but one word from you will silence me forever. If, however, your feelings have changed, I will have to tell you: you have bewitched me, body and soul, and I love, I love, I love you. I never wish to be parted from you from this day on."

Mr. Darcy, *Pride & Prejudice* (2005)

"I wish I knew how to quit you."

Jack Twist, *Brokeback Mountain* (2005)

"Two weeks together, that's all it took, two weeks for me to fall in love with you."

Savannah Curtis, *Dear John* (2010)

"She was Lo, plain Lo, in the morning, standing four feet ten in one sock. She was Lola in slacks, she was Dolly at school. She was Dolores on the dotted line. But in my arms she was always - Lolita. Light of my life, fire of my loins. My sin. My soul."

Humbert, *Lolita* (1997)

"You should be kissed every day, every hour, every minute."

Logan, *The Lucky One* (2012)

"Because the truth is, Sophie, I am madly, truly, deeply, passionately in love with you."

Charlie, *Letters to Juliet* (2010)

"So Margaret, marry me, because I'd like to date you."

Andrew Paxton, *The Proposal* (2009)

"Have you never met a woman who inspires you to love? Until your every sense is filled with her? You inhale her. You taste her. You see your unborn children in her eyes and know that your heart has at last found a home. Your life begins with her, and without her it must surely end."

Don Juan, *Don Juan DeMarco* (1994)

"It seems right now that all I've ever done in my life is making my way here to you."

Robert, *The Bridges of Madison County* (1995)

"The best love is the kind that awakens the soul and makes us reach for more, that plants a fire in our hearts and brings peace to our minds, and that's what you've given me."

Noah, *The Notebook* (2004)

"Death cannot stop true love. All it can do is delay it for a while."

Westley, *The Princess Bride* (1987)

"Of all the gin joints, in all the towns, in all the world, she walks into mine."

Rick, *Casablanca* (1942)

"If I could ask God one thing, it would be to stop the moon. Stop the moon and make this night and your beauty last forever."

William, *A Knight's Tale* (2001)

"I've already wasted my whole life. I want to tell you with my last breath that I have always loved you. I would rather be a ghost, drifting by your side as a condemned soul, than enter heaven without you. Because of your love, I will never be a lonely spirit."

Li Mu Bai, *Crouching Tiger, Hidden Dragon* (2000)

"Well, it was a million tiny little things that, when you added them all up, they meant we were supposed to be together... and I knew it. I knew it the very first time I touched her. It was like coming home... only to no home I'd ever known... I was just taking her hand to help her out of a car and I knew. It was like... magic."

Sam Baldwin, *Sleepless in Seattle* (1993)

"New lovers are nervous and tender, but smash everything. For the heart is an organ of fire."

Almasy, *The English Patient* (1996)

"You're not perfect, sport, and let me save you the suspense: this girl you've met, she's not perfect either. But the question is whether or not you're perfect for each other."

Sean, *Good Will Hunting* (1997)

"I have crossed oceans of time to find you."

Dracula, *Dracula* (1992)

"Love means never having to say you're sorry."

Oliver Barrett IV, *Love Story* (1970)

Daisy: Would you still love me if I were old and saggy?

Benjamin Button: Would you still love ME if I were young and had acne? When I'm afraid of what's under the stairs? Or if I end up wetting the bed?

The Curious Case of Benjamin Button (2008)

"I love you. You're my only reason to stay alive... if that's what I am."

Edward Cullen, *The Twilight Saga: New Moon* (2009)

"Listen to me, mister. You're my knight in shining armor. Don't forget it. You're going to get back on that horse and I'm going to be right behind you, holding on tight and away we're going to go, go, go!"

Ethel, *On Golden Pond* (1981)

Jamie: [in English] It's my favorite time of day, driving you.

Aurelia: [in Portuguese] It's the saddest part of my day, leaving you.

Love Actually (2003)

"No, you submit, do you hear? You be strong, you survive... You stay alive, no matter what occurs! I will find you. No matter how long it takes, no matter how far, I will find you."

Hawkeye, *The Last of the Mohicans* (1992)

"As you wish."

Westley, *The Princess Bride* (1987)

"I love that you get cold when it's 71 degrees out. I love that it takes you an hour and a half to order a sandwich. I love that you get a little crinkle above your nose when you're looking at me like I'm nuts. I love that after I spend the day with you, I can still smell your perfume on my clothes. And I love that you are the last person I want to talk to before I go to sleep at night. And it's not because I'm lonely, and it's not because it's New Year's Eve. I came here tonight because when you realize you want to spend the rest of your life with somebody, you want the rest of your life to start as soon as possible."

Harry Burns, *When Harry Met Sally* (1989)

"Isabella Swan, I promise to love you every moment of forever. Would you do me the extraordinary honor of marrying me?"

Edward Cullen, *The Twilight Saga: Eclipse* (2010)

Mark: But for now, let me say - Without hope or agenda - Just because it's Christmas - And at Christmas you tell the truth - To me, you are perfect - And my wasted heart will love you - Until you look like this.

[picture of a mummy]

Mark: Merry Christmas.

Love Actually (2003)

"We'll always have Paris."

Casablanca (1942)

"Michael, I love you. I've loved you for nine years. I've just been too arrogant and scared to realize it, and, well, now, I'm just scared, so - I-I-I realize this comes at a very inopportune time, but I really have this gigantic favor to ask of you. Choose me. M-marry me. Let me make you happy. Oh, that sounds like three favors, doesn't it? B-but..."

Julianne Potter, *My Best Friend's Wedding* (1997)

"I wanted it to be you. I wanted it to be you so badly."

Kathleen Kelly, *You've Got Mail* (1998)

"I know it's a cornball thing, but love is passion. Obsession. Someone you can't live without. I say fall head over heels. Find someone you can love like crazy, and who'll love you the same way back. How do you you find 'em? Well, you forget your head and you listen to your heart. I'm not hearing any heart. Because the truth is, honey, there's no sense living your life without this. To make the journey and not fall deeply in love, well, you haven't lived a life at all. But you have to try, because if you haven't tried, you haven't lived."

William Parish, *Meet Joe Black* (1998)

"You're a beautiful woman, you deserve a beautiful life. Nothing less."

Jacob, *Water for Elephants* (2011)

"I promise, I'll come back for you. I promise, I'll never leave you."

Almasy, *The English Patient* (1996)

"And maybe it'll be enough if you know that in the few hours we had together we loved a lifetime's worth."

Sarah, *The Terminator* (1984)

"You're the first boy I ever kissed, Jake, and I want you to be the last."

Melanie Carmichael, *Sweet Home Alabama* (2002)

"I will have poetry in my life. And adventure. And love. Love above all. No... not the artful postures of love, not playful and poetical games of love for the amusement of an evening. but love that...overthrows life. Unbiddable, ungovernable, like a riot in the heart, and nothing to be done, come ruin or rapture."

Viola, *Shakespeare in Love* (1998)

"You said you couldn't be with someone who didn't believe in you. Well I believed in you. I just didn't believe in me. I love you... always."

Blane, *Pretty in Pink* (1986)

Sara: You don't have to understand. You just have to have faith.

Jonathan: Faith in what?

Sara: Destiny

Serendipity (2001)

"Love's involved with spending time together, but spending time apart, can lead to loving even more."

Tyler, *Remember me* (2010)

"I love you without knowing how, or when, or from where. I love you straightforwardly without complexities or pride. I love you because I know no other way then this. So close that your hand, on my chest, is my hand. So close, that when you close your eyes, I fall asleep."

Hunter Patch Adams, *Patch Adams* (1998)

"It's like seeing someone for the first time, and you look at each other for a few seconds, and there's this kind of recognition like you both know something. Next moment the person's gone, and it's too late to do anything about it."

Jack Foley, *Out of Sight* (1998)

"Life is not the amount of breaths you take, it's the moments that take your breath away."

Hitch, *Hitch* (2005)

"Since we have been together I have felt more uncomfortable, out of place, embarassed, and just physically sick then I have in my entire life. But I could not have gone through that, I could not have thrown up 19 times in 48 days if I was not in love with you."

Reuben Feffer, *Along Came Polly* (2004)

"Why don't you come up some time and see me?"

Lady Lou, *She Done Him Wrong* (1933)

"I'm not a smart man... but I know what love is."

Forrest Gump, *Forrest Gump* (1994)

"I don't know who you are, Henry...but I dream about you almost every night."

Lucy, *50 First Dates* (2004)

"Good luck finding somebody to put up with your shit for more than, like, six months. Okay? But I accept the whole package, the crazy and the brilliant. Alright? I know you're not gonna change and I don't want you to. It's called accepting you for being you."

Jesse, *Before Midnight* (2013)

"I am in love with you. And I know that love is just a shout into the void, and that oblivion is inevitable, and that we're all doomed, and that one day all of our labors will be returned to dust. And I know that the sun will swallow the only Earth we will ever have. And I am in love with you."

Gus, *The Fault in our Stars* (2014)

"Oh, it's nobody's fault but my own! I was looking up... it was the nearest thing to heaven! You were there..."

Terry McKay, *An Affair to Remember* (1957)

"Here's looking at you, kid."

Rick, *Casablanca* (1942)

Watts: [putting on Keith's diamond earrings] What do you think?

Keith: You look good wearing my future.

Some Kind of Wonderful (1987)

Katie: Wouldn't it be lovely if we were old? We'd have survived all this. Everything thing would be easy and uncomplicated; the way it was when we were young.

Hubbell: Katie, it was never uncomplicated.

The Way We Were (1973)

"Let's just say in some alternate universe, there's a couple just like us, okay? Only she's healthy and he's perfect. And their world is about how much they're going to spend on vacation or who's in a bad mood that day, or whether they feel guilty about having a cleaning lady. I don't want to be those people. I want us. You. This."

Jamie Randall, *Love & Other Drugs* (2010)

"Winning that ticket, Rose, was the best thing that ever happened to me… it brought me to you. And I'm thankful for that, Rose. I'm thankful. You must do me this honor. Promise me you'll survive. That you won't give up, no matter what happens, no matter how hopeless. Promise me now, Rose, and never let go of that promise."

Jack Dawson, Titanic (1997)

BOOKS
ROMANTIC LINES

"We would be together and have our books and at night be warm in bed together with the windows open and the stars bright."

- Ernest Hemingway, *A Moveable Feast*

"I'm in love with you, and I'm not in the business of denying myself the simple pleasure of saying true things. I'm in love with you, and I know that love is just a shout into the void, and that oblivion is inevitable, and that we're all doomed and that there will come a day when all our labor has been returned to dust, and I know the sun will swallow the only earth we'll ever have, and I am in love with you."

– John Green, *The Fault in our Stars*

"I want everyone to meet you. You're my favorite person of all time."

- Rainbow Rowell, *Eleanor and Park*

"If my love were an ocean,
there would be no more land.
If my love were a desert,
you would see only sand.
If my love were a star-
late at night, only light.
And if my love could grow
wings,
I'd be soaring in flight."

– Jay Asher, *Thirteen Reasons Why*

"He stepped down, trying not to look long at her, as if she were the sun, yet he saw her, like the sun, even without looking."

- Leo Tolstoy, *Anna Karenina*

"She will lose her innocence. She will see me again and I will find nothing but indifference. I helped another woman."

- John Castle, *Living in Sin*

"You should be kissed and often, and by someone who knows how."

- Margaret Mitchell, *Gone With the Wind*

"When you fall in love, it is a temporary madness. It erupts like an earthquake, and then it subsides. And when it subsides, you have to make a decision. You have to work out whether your roots are to become so entwined together that it is inconceivable that you should ever part. Because this is what love is. Love is not breathlessness, it is not excitement, it is not the desire to mate every second of the day. It is not lying awake at night imagining that he is kissing every part of your body. No ... don't blush. I am telling you some truths. For that is just being in love; which any of us can convince ourselves we are. Love itself is what is left over, when being in love has burned away. Doesn't sound very exciting, does it? But it is!"

- Louis de Bernières, *Captain Corelli's Mandolin*

"It was love at first sight, at last sight, at ever and ever sight."

- Vladimir Nabokov, *Lolita*

"She sat leaning back in her chair, looking ahead, knowing that he was as aware of her as she was of him. She found pleasure in the special self-consciousness it gave her. When she crossed her legs, when she leaned on her arm against the window sill, when she brushed her hair off her forehead – every movement of her body was underscored by a feeling the unadmitted words for which were: Is he seeing it?"

- Ayn Rand, *Atlas Shrugged*

"You pierce my soul. I am half agony, half hope. Tell me not that I am too late, that such precious feelings are gone for ever. I offer myself to you again with a heart even more your own than when you almost broke it, eight years and a half ago. Dare not say that man forgets sooner than woman, that his love has an earlier death. I have loved none but you."

- Jane Austen, *Persuasion*

"I wish I knew how to quit you."

- Annie Proulx, *Brokeback Mountain*

"She is a mortal danger to all men. She is beautiful without knowing it, and possesses charms that she's not even aware of. She is like a trap set by nature - a sweet perfumed rose in whose petals Cupid lurks in ambush! Anyone who has seen her smile has known perfection. She instills grace in every common thing and divinity in every careless gesture. Venus in her shell was never so lovely, and Diana in the forest never so graceful as my Lady when she strides through Paris!"

- Edmond Rostand, *Cyrano De Bergerac*

"I want to do with you what spring does with the cherry trees."

- Pablo Neruda, *Twenty Love Poems and a Song of Despair*

"To love or have loved, that is enough. Ask nothing further. There is no other pearl to be found in the dark folds of life."

- Victor Hugo, *Les Misérables*

"I am nothing special; just a common man with common thoughts, and I've led a common life. There are no monuments dedicated to me and my name will soon be forgotten. But in one respect I have succeeded as gloriously as anyone who's ever lived: I've loved another with all my heart and soul; and to me, this has always been enough."

- Nicholas Sparks, *The Notebook*

"By my soul, I can neither eat, drink, nor sleep; nor, what's still worse, love any woman in the world but her."

- Samuel Richardson, *Clarissa, or The History of a Young Lady*

"...I fell in love the way you fall asleep: slowly, and then all at once."

- John Green, *The Fault in Our Stars*

"You and I, it's as though we have been taught to kiss in heaven and sent down to earth together, to see if we know what we were taught."

- Boris Pasternak, *Doctor Zhivago*

"Deep in the meadow, hidden far away
A cloak of leaves, a moonbeam ray
Forget your woes and let your troubles lay
And when it's morning again, they'll wash away
Here it's safe, here it's warm
Here the daisies guard you from every harm
Here your dreams are sweet and tomorrow brings them true
Here is the place where I love you."

- Suzanne Collins, *The Hunger Games*

"In vain I have struggled. It will not do. My feelings will not be repressed. You must allow me to tell you how ardently I admire and love you."

- Jane Austen, *Pride and Prejudice*

"I have waited for this opportunity for more than half a century, to repeat to you once again my vow of eternal fidelity and everlasting love."

- Gabriel García Márquez, *Love in the Time of Cholera*

"…the friendship I have had in my heart for you has ripened into a deeper feeling, a feeling more beautiful, more pure, more sacred. Dare I name it you? Ah! It is love which makes me so bold!"

- Margaret Mitchell, *Gone with the Wind*

"Love, it is said, is blind, but love is not blind. It is an extra eye, which shows us what is most worthy of regard. To see the best is to see most clearly, and it is the lover's privilege."

- J.M. Barrie, *The Little Minister*

"Whatever our souls are made of, his and mine are the same."

- Emily Brontë, *Wuthering Heights*

"Now, I'm not going to deny that I was aware of your beauty. But the point is, this has nothing to do with your beauty. As I got to know you, I began to realise that beauty was the least of your qualities. I became fascinated by your goodness. I was drawn in by it. I didn't understand what was happening to me. And it was only when I began to feel actual, physical pain every time you left the room that it finally dawned on me: I was in love, for the first time in my life. I knew it was hopeless, but that didn't matter to me. And it's not that I want to have you. All I want is to deserve you. Tell me what to do. Show me how to behave. I'll do anything you say."

- Choderlos de Laclos, *Dangerous Liaisons*

"So, I love you because the entire universe conspired to help me find you."

- Paulo Coelho, The Alchemist

"All hopes of eternity and all gain from the past he would have given to have her there, to be wrapped warm with him in one blanket, and sleep, only sleep. It seemed the sleep with the woman in his arms was the only necessity."

- D.H. Lawrence, *Lady Chatterley's Lover*

"All this gladness in life, all honest pride in doing my work in the world, all this keen sense of being, I owe to her!" And it doubles the gladness, it makes the pride glow, it sharpens the sense of existence till I hardly know if it is pain or pleasure, to think that I owe it to one - nay, you must, you shall hear" - said he, stepping forwards with stern determination - "to one whom I love, as I do not believe man ever loved woman before."

- Elizabeth Gaskell, *North and South*

"I cannot fix on the hour, or the look, or the words, which laid the foundation. It was too long ago. I was in the middle before I knew that I had begun."

- Jane Austen, *Pride and Prejudice*

"You can give without loving, but you can never love without giving. The great acts of love are done by those who are habitually performing small acts of kindness. We pardon to the extent that we love. Love is knowing that even when you are alone, you will never be lonely again. And great happiness of life is the conviction that we are loved. Loved for ourselves. & even loved in spite of ourselves."

- Victor Hugo, *Les Miserables*

"Love had caught him out of triviality and Maurice out of bewilderment in order that two imperfect souls might touch perfection."

- E.M. Forster, *Maurice*

"Soul meets soul on lovers' lips."

- Percy Bysshe Shelley, *Prometheus Unbound*

"He knew that when he kissed this girl, and forever wed his unutterable visions to her perishable breath, his mind would never romp again like the mind of God. So he waited, listening for a moment longer to the tuning-fork that had been struck upon a star. Then he kissed her. At his lips' touch she blossomed for him like a flower and the incarnation was complete."

- F. Scott Fitzgerald, *The Great Gatsby*

"'Tis better to have loved and lost, Than never to have loved at all."

- Alfred Lord Tennyson, *In Memoriam A.H.H.*

"You know what I am going to say. I love you. What other men may mean when they use that expression, I cannot tell; what I mean is, that I am under the influence of some tremendous attraction which I have resisted in vain, and which overmasters me. You could draw me to fire, you could draw me to water, you could draw me to the gallows, you could draw me to any death, you could draw me to anything I have most avoided, you could draw me to any exposure and disgrace. This and the confusion of my thoughts, so that I am fit for nothing, is what I mean by your being the ruin of me. But if you would return a favourable answer to my offer of myself in marringe, you could draw me to any good - every good - with equal force."

- Charles Dickens, *Our Mutual Friend*

"I don't ask you to love me always like this, but I ask you to remember. Somewhere inside me there'll always be the person I am to-night."

- F Scott Fitzgerald, *Tender is the Night*

"I cannot let you burn me up, nor can I resist you. No mere human can stand in a fire and not be consumed."

- A.S. Byatt, *Possesion*

"It has made me better loving you ... it has made me wiser, and easier, and brighter. I used to want a great many things before, and to be angry that I did not have them. Theoretically, I was satisfied. I flattered myself that I had limited my wants. But I was subject to irritation; I used to have morbid sterile hateful fits of hunger, of desire. Now I really am satisfied, because I can't think of anything better."

- Henry James, *The Portrait of a Lady*

"I have a million things to talk to you about. All I want in this world is you. I want to see you and talk. I want the two of us to begin everything from the beginning."

- Haruki Murakami, *Norwegian Wood*

"Grow old along with me! The best is yet to be."

- Robert Browning, *Rabbi Ben Ezra*

"Lying under such a myriad of stars. The sea's black horizon. He rose and walked out and stood barefoot in the sand and watched the pale surf appear all down the shore and roll and crash and darken again. When he went back to the fire he knelt and smoothed her hair as she slept and he said if he were God he would have made the world just so and no different."

- Cormac Mccarthy, *The Road*

"I loved her against reason, against promise, against peace, against hope, against happiness, against all discouragement that could be."

- Charles Dickens, *Great Expectations*

"One hour of right down love is worth an age of dully living on."

- Aphra Benn, *The Rover*

"The power of a glance has been so much abused in love stories, that it has come to be disbelieved in. Few people dare now to say that two beings have fallen in love because they have looked at each other. Yet it is in this way that love begins, and in this way only."

- Victor Hugo, *Les Miserables*

"I must, then, repeat continually that we are forever sundered – and yet, while I breathe and think, I must love him."

- Charlotte Brontë, *Jane Eyre*

"Oh the heart that has truly loved never forgets, But as truly loves on to the close."

- Thomas Moore, *Believe Me, If All Those Endearing Young Charms*

"I wanted so badly to lie down next to her on the couch, to wrap my arms around her and sleep. Not fuck, like in those movies. Not even have sex. Just sleep together in the most innocent sense of the phrase."

John Green, *Looking for Alaska*

"It is better to love wisely, no doubt: but to love foolishly is better than not to be able to love at all."

-       William   Makepeace Thackeray, *Vanity Fair*

"Doubt thou the stars are fire; Doubt that the sun doth move; Doubt truth to be a liar; But never doubt I love."

- William Shakespeare, *Hamlet*

"If you live to be a hundred, I want to live to be a hundred minus one day, so I never have to live without you."

- A.A. Milne, *Winnie the Pooh*

"She is a friend of mind. She gather me, man. The pieces I am, she gather them and give them back to me in all the right order. It's good, you know, when you got a woman who is a friend of your mind."

- Toni Morrison, *Beloved*

"Did my heart love till now? Forswear it, sight! For I ne'er saw true beauty till this night."

- William Shakespeare, *Romeo and Juliet*

"What greater thing is there for two human souls, than to feel that they are joined for life--to strengthen each other in all labour, to rest on each other in all sorrow, to minister to each other in all pain, to be one with each other in silent unspeakable memories at the moment of the last parting?"

- George Eliot, *Adam Bede*

"O, my luve's like a red, red rose,
That's newly sprung in June."

- Robert Burns, *My Luve is Like a Red Red Rose*

"Every atom of your flesh is as dear to me as my own: in pain and sickness it would still be dear."

- Charlotte Brontë, *Jane Eyre*

"You are my heart, my life, my one and only thought."

- Arthur Conan Doyle, *The White Company*

"Each time you happen to me all over again."

- Edith Wharton, *The Age of Innocence*

"The way her body existed only where he touched her. The rest of her was smoke."

- Arundhati Roy, *The God of Small Things*

"It is not time or opportunity that is to determine intimacy; - it is disposition alone. Seven years would be insufficient to make some people acquainted with each other, and seven days are more than enough for others."

- Jane Austen, *Sense and Sensibility*

"The winds were warm about us, the whole earth seemed the wealthier for our love."

- Harriet Prescott Spofford, *The Amber Gods*

"She was more than human to me. She was a Fairy, a Sylph, I don't know what she was - anything that no one ever saw, and everything that everybody ever wanted. I was swallowed up in an abyss of love in an instant. There was no pausing on the brink; no looking down, or looking back; I was gone, headlong, before I had sense to say a word to her."

- Charles Dickens, *David Copperfield*

"Her life with others no longer interests him. He wants only her stalking beauty, her theatre of expressions. He wants the minute secret reflection between them, the depth of field minimal, their foreignness intimate like two pages of a closed book."

- Michael Ondaatje, *The English Patient*

"Her love was entire as a child's, and though warm as summer it was fresh as spring."

- Thomas Hardy, *Far From the Madding Crowd*

"That the last two letters in her name were the first two in his, a silly thing he never mentioned to her but caused him to believe that they were bound together."

- Jhumpa Lahiri, *Unaccustomed Earth*

"Love seeketh not itself to please, Nor for itself hath any care; But for another gives its ease, And builds a Heaven in Hell's despair."

- William Blake, *The Clod and the Pebble*

"He feeds upon her face by day and night, And she with true kind eyes looks back on him, Fair as the moon and joyful as the light."

- Christina Rossetti, *In an Artist's Studio*

"If all else perished, and he remained, I should still continue to be; and if all else remained, and he were annihilated, the universe would turn to a mighty stranger: I should not seem apart of it."
- Emily Brontë, *Wuthering Heights*

"Is it that happy stretch of time when the lovers set to chronicling their passion. When no glance, no tone of voice is so fleeting but it shines with significance. When each moment, each perception is brought out with care, unfolded like a precious gem from its layers of the softest tissue paper and laid in front of the beloved - turned this way and that, examined, considered."

- Ahdaf Soueif, *The Map of Love*

"I've never had a moment's doubt. I love you. I believe in you completely. You are my dearest one. My reason for life."

- Ian McEwan, *Atonement*

"Before you, Bella, my life was like a moonless night. Very dark, but there were stars — points of light and reason. ...And then you shot across my sky like a meteor. Suddenly everything was on fire; there was brilliancy, there was beauty. When you were gone, when the meteor had fallen over the horizon, everything went black. Nothing had changed, but my eyes were blinded by the light. I couldn't see the stars anymore. And there was no more reason for anything."

- Stephenie Meyer, *New Moon*

"Once upon a time there was a boy who loved a girl, and her laughter was a question he wanted to spend his whole life answering"

- Nicole Krauss , *The History of Love*

"She wasn't doing a thing that I could see, except leaning there on the balcony railing, holding the universe together."

J D Salinger, *A Girl I Knew*

"I'm in love with you, and I know that love is just a shout into the void, and that oblivion is inevitable, and that we're all doomed and that there will come a day when all our labor has been returned to dust, and I know the sun will swallow the only earth we'll ever have, and I am in love with you."

- John Green, *The Fault in Our Stars*

"But soft! What light through yonder window breaks? It is the east and Juliet is the sun."

- William Shakespeare, *Romeo and Juliet*

"He was my North, my South, my East and West,
My working week and my Sunday rest,
My noon, my midnight, my talk, my song;
I thought that love would last forever: I was wrong."

- W.H. Auden, *Collected Poems*

"Day before yesterday I saw a rabbit, and yesterday a deer, and today, you."

- Robert F. Young, *The Dandelion Girl*

"I love the ground under his feet, and the air over his head, and everything he touches and every word he says. I love all his looks, and all his actions and him entirely and all together."

- Emily Brontë, *Wuthering Heights*

"But to see her was to love her,
Love but her, and love forever.
Had we never lou'd sae kindly,
Had we never lou'd sae blindly,
Never met - or never parted -
We had ne'er been broken hearted"

- Robert Burns, *Robert Burns*

"He was now in that state of fire that she loved. She wanted to be burnt."

- Anaïs Nin, *Delta of Venus*

"She is all the great heroines of the world in one. She is more than an individual. I love her, and I must make her love me. I want to make Romeo jealous. I want the dead lovers of the world to hear our laughter, and grow sad. I want a breath of our passion to stir dust into consciousness, to wake their ashes into pain. "

- Oscar Wilde, *The Picture of Dorian Gray*

"The smell of her hair, the taste of her mouth, the feeling of her skin seemed to have got inside him, or into the air all round him. She had become a physical necessity."

- George Orwell, *1984*

"She is a mortal danger to all men. She is beautiful without knowing it, and possesses charms that she's not even aware of. She is like a trap set by nature – a sweet perfumed rose in whose petals Cupid lurks in ambush! Anyone who has seen her smile has known perfection. She instills grace in every common thing and divinity in every careless gesture. Venus in her shell was never so lovely, and Diana in the forest never so graceful as my Lady when she strides through Paris!"

- Edmond Rostand, *Cyrano de Bergerac*

"My bounty is as boundless as the sea, my love as deep. The more I give thee, the more I have, for both are infinite."

- William Shakespeare, *Romeo and Juliet*

ROMANTIC PICK-UP LINES

You are so beautiful that you give the sun a reason to shine.

I just wanted to show this rose how incredibly beautiful you are!

The only thing your eyes haven't told me is your name.

Sorry lady, but you owe me a drink. Because when I looked at you, I dropped mine.

I think I can die happy now, coz I've just seen a piece of heaven.

Your eyes are as dark as a castle moat by midnight. Lower your drawbridge and let me cross.

You must be a magician, because every time I look at you, everyone else disappears.

I don't mean to bother you, but I had to come over and introduce my self; otherwise I'll be kicking myself for days.

I'm no organ donor, but I'd be happy to give you my heart.

Kissing you is like Drinking salty water: You drink, but then your thirst only increases.

Excuse me. I'm writing an essay on the finer things in life, and I was wondering if I could interview you.

Honey always remember, it's not who you are, or what I am, it's what we become whem we are together

If I had a rose for every time I thought of you, I would be walking through my garden forever.

When I tell you I love you, I don't say it out of habit. I say it to remind you that you are the best thing that has ever happend to me

I wish I was one of your tears, so I could be born in your eyes, run down your cheek, and die on your lips.

In a relationship, I only want three things: eyes that won't cry, lips that won't lie, and love that won't die.

Can you give me directions to your heart? I've seemed to have lost myself in your eyes.

Of all the beautiful curves on your body, your smile is my favorite.

It's not my fault I fell in love. You are the one that tripped me.

God gave us two ears, two eyes, two legs and two hands, but he only gave us one heart, and he wanted me to find you and tell you, you are the second one.

This morning I saw a flower and I thought it was the most beautiful thing I've ever seen; until I met you.

I know somebody who likes you but if I weren't so shy, I'd tell you who.

Was your father a thief? 'Cause someone stole the stars from the sky and put them in your eyes.

Me without you is like a nerd without braces, A shoe without laces,
aSentenceWithoutSpaces.

I thought happiness started with an H. Why does mine start with U?

If I received a nickel for everytime I saw someone as beautiful as you, I'd have five cents.

There are many fish in the sea but you're the only one that's caught my eye.

When I'm older looking back at all of my finest memories, and I'll think of the day my children were born, the day I got married, and the day that I met you.

If LOVE was written on every grain of sand in the Sahara Desert that still doesn't equal my love for you.

If you wake up in a red room with no windows or doors, don't be alarmed, you're just in my heart.

I don't know which is prettier today, the water, the sky or your eyes.

I think you've got something in your eye. Oh never mind, it's just a sparkle.

Did the sun come up or did you just smile at me?

Do you know what I did last night? I looked up at the stars, and matched each one with a reason why I love you

I can't think of anyone else I'd rather survive a Zombie Apocalypse with.

If a star fell for every time I thought of you, the sky would be empty.

I just have to say this, because honesty is the best policy. You are the most beautiful woman I've ever seen!

If I had to choose between breathing and loving you, I'd take my last breath to say I love you.

Ever wonder why you have spaces between your fingers? So my fingers can fit there.

Hi, my friend thinks you're kinda cute, but I don't. I think you're absolutely gorgeous.

Before I met you I never knew what it was like to be able to look at someone and smile for no reason

No man is worth your tears, but once you find one that is, he won't make you cry.

I was gonna say something really sweet about you but when I saw you I was speechless.

Because of you, I laugh a little harder, cry a little less, and smile a lot more.

If I walked a millimeter for every time I thought of you, I would have walked across the Earth a million times.

You look like the morning sun after a long night of darkness.

If I had a dollar for every time I thought of you, I'd only have a dollar because you never leave my mind.

You stole my heart. Can I steal your last name?

Why do you have to be so damn fine every single day? Can't you take a break and let me concentrate on something else for a change?

If beauty were time, you'd be an eternity.

I tried to find the perfect line to make you mine, sweetheart, but after searching all I could come up with was this look in my eyes and your hand in mine, and the words, will you be mine?

Excuse me, can you empty your pockets? I believe you have stolen my heart.

My recipe for love is one cup of you, one cup of me, knead till hard, and serve hot.

You know, you might be asked to leave soon. You're making the other women look really bad.

I now believe in Angels. Do you believe in fate?

If you had eleven roses and you looked in the mirror; then you'd see twelve of the most beautiful things in the world.

Excuse me, I just noticed you noticing me and I just wanted to give you notice that I noticed you too.

It took three tries to approach you. I kept losing my breath.

If I were a stop light, I'd turn red every time you passed by just for the chance to stare at you longer

Can I borrow a quarter? So I can call my mom and tell her I just met the girl of my dreams.

Can I take your picture to prove to my friends that angels do exist?

We're like a 4-Leaf clover. You're the C and I'm the R, and there's love in between us.

Hey, don't frown. You never know who could be falling for your smile.

Your heart stops when you sneeze. Kind of like what happens when I think of you.

Close your eyes. What do you see? That's my life without you.

OTHER
ROMANTIC LINES

"You know you're in love when you can't fall asleep because reality is finally better than your dreams."

- Dr. Seuss

"For you see, each day I love you more
Today more than yesterday and less than tomorrow."

- Rosemonde Gérard

"Love never dies a natural death. It dies because we don't know how to replenish its source. It dies of blindness and errors and betrayals. It dies of illness and wounds; it dies of weariness, of witherings, of tarnishings."

- Anaïs Nin

"One word frees us of all the weight and pain of life: That word is love."

- Sophocles

"The real lover is the man who can thrill you by kissing your forehead or smiling into your eyes or just staring into space."

- Marilyn Monroe

"Any man who can drive safely while kissing a pretty girl is simply not giving the kiss the attention it deserves."

- Albert Einstein

"You don't love someone for their looks, or their clothes or for their fancy car, but because they sing a song only you can hear."

- Oscar Wilde

"We loved with a love that was more than love."

-Edgar Allan Poe

"Actually, there is a word for that. It's love. I'm in love with her, okay? If you're looking for the word that means caring about someone beyond all rationality and wanting them to have everything they want no matter how much it destroys you, it's love. And when you love someone you just, you...you don't stop, ever. Even when people roll their eyes, and call you crazy. Even then. Especially then. You just– you don't give up. Because if I could just give up...if I could just, you know, take the whole world's advice and– and move on and find someone else, that wouldn't be love. That would be... that would be some other disposable thing that is not worth fighting for. But I– that is not what this is."

-Ted, How I Met Your Mother

"When I say, 'I love you,' it's not because I want you or because I can't have you. It has nothing to do with me. I love what you are, what you do, how you try. I've seen your kindness and your strength. I've seen the best and the worst of you. And I understand with perfect clarity exactly what you are. You're a hell of a woman."

Spike, Buffy the Vampire Slayer

Chuck: Your world would be easier if I didn't come back.

Blair: That's true but it wouldn't be my world without you in it.

Gossip Girl

uncrackedballs@gmail.com

Books on Dating

Romantic Movies

Romance Books

Love Quotes

Romantic Quotes

Books on Relationships

Dating and Relationship

Books on Love and Relationships

Amazon Prime Books to Borrow for Free

Books on Sale

Lending Library for Prime Members

Top 100 Best Sellers in Kindle Books

Nonfiction Best Sellers 2014

New Book Releases

Kindle Books Best Seller

Amazon Prime Ebooks

Kindle Unlimited

Books to Borrow free with Amazon Prime

www.ingramcontent.com/pod-product-compliance
Lightning Source LLC
Chambersburg PA
CBHW050435290526
45786CB00006B/2044